Entropia

Entropia

Kadambari Baxi and Reinhold Martin

Contents

Introduction

The future was yesterday. What remains is to escape it. Entropia then, is already here: a hole in yesterday's future. It is a falsification, an artificial repetition.

Tiny sequences are excerpted from the architectural genome, tampered with, and reinserted. The effect, however, is not an accelerated evolution toward an open future, but an accelerated devolution into an indeterminate present. This present is inaccessible as such, appearing only through the mediation of past/future combinations and hence, recombinations. Under such conditions all projections, favorable or unfavorable, become symptoms, or rather, symptoms of symptoms. Utopia and dystopia require and reproduce one another, in inverted form. Together, they measure the emptiness of the present. Entropia locates itself within this emptiness without remorse. The respective violence of past and future is there for all to see. The compulsion to recover apocryphal wholenesses or to consolidate future multiplicities becomes fully automated and without meaning.

It is a familiar landscape, awash in partnerships between corporate and civil societies, between foreign and domestic agencies. In the face of these new organisms – whose sales pitch rings of the avant-garde: "hybridity will set you free" – stand the ominous figures of the natural community, the national soul, and the unified subject, all regressive responses to the alienation and disaggregation heralded by undreamed-of mutations. But it is not that modernity's latest turn is hopelessly alienating; it is that it is not alienating enough. The more things are torn apart the more they are forced together, compulsively reconnected into fantasmatic unities. And so precisely transparency, that hallmark of visionary modernisms, has again become inseparable from fantasies of seamless integration: transparency of home to office, of private to public, of nation to corporation – utopias, and therefore dystopias, of transparent communication.

In Entropia, the signal to noise ratio – index of communicative transparency – is always less than one. Which means that pattern is always largely obscured, interfered with. The precise location of Entropia can therefore never be pinpointed, its borders never quite confirmed. It may or may not be where you think it is.

Its building blocks are the units scrambled and rescrambled by modernity's fluxions. A sampling includes a homeoffice, an open house, and an embassy without a territory. Like all conceivable components of Entropia, each of these in some sense contains the others. This is

Entropia's topology: a cascade of outsides within insides – impacted, collapsed, porous. Home and office, private and public, foreign and domestic do not so much interpenetrate as erase one another from an inside which is always in the process of becoming an outside. In other words, your roof leaks, or, you find holes in your soul.

And so the architecture of Entropia can never be thought autonomously. It engulfs, surrounds and inhales itself, and with itself, the world. Likewise the world, Entropia, passes through architecture. This is not a question of "context" – discursive, cultural, or physical. It is a question of what used to be called the "constituent facts" of an epoch, stripped of their powers of causality and reactivated as raw material, input.

In this sense and many others, the status of architecture in Entropia is that of one among many media. Tired incantations invoking digital novelty are countered with both sensory deprivation and information overload: kaleidoscope, cacophony, and silence. The from-to of the assembly line is converted into the circularity of mediatic interchangeability. From real buildings to real (that is, digital) models to images – real images, derived from a real architecture, set into real (that is, digital) motion and combined with moving images, excerpted from real films, with real words and real (that is, digital) sounds. This is the architecture of Entropia, an architecture through which architecture itself incessantly passes.

Each of the three objects that follow is thus inseparable from its multiple functions within this mediatic circuit, of which this book in turn forms one link. Outside of this book, these objects are assimilated into an interactive digital projection via the animation of the still images presented here, combined with cinematic fragments, advertisements, news footage, and text. The result, which is documented with each project, is not the revitalization of the flat two-dimensionality of the page or the screen with sound and motion, but rather, its further desiccation. Three-dimensionality continues to flatten out as processes of indefinite duration, such as the blurring of the image and consequent dissipation of the perspectival effect, are set into motion automatically and programmed to stop only with the intervention of the user. Click. All interactions (click) lead, eventually, to the same place. The dream of nonlinearity is thus confronted with the overdeterminations of "choice".

Entropia's raw material is all drawn from a period spanning from the late 1950s to just after the end of the Vietnam War. It was a period when the technologized violence of the Cold War was heated up to the point of meltdown, over which were superimposed old utopias of communication – updated to include the new machinery – that exhausted themselves in the streets, the battlefield, and the corridors of the Watergate complex. Entropia replays this exhaustion, introducing indefinite pauses, infinite loops, and closed circuits into the relentless forward-march toward a vacant, violent future, so that something other may stand a chance of being allowed in, or out.

Homeoffice

A modern skyscraper is reprogrammed and subjected to a process of skin replacement. An example of the increasingly obsolete architecture of 1960s office buildings, the First City National Bank in Houston, Texas, by Gordon Bunshaft of Skidmore, Owings & Merrill (1961), is selected for metamorphosis. The result is a spatialized blur.

The SOM building, standing on the threshold of the heavy new structuralisms of the 1960s, is chosen for its clarity of purpose. The frame is "expressed" on the outside in order to minimize its effect on the interior. This building thus deploys its modernist structural rationalism as a corporate logo: the architectural "real" (structure) as image (skin). Whereas it is clear today that the rigid grid, formerly the very emblem of capitalist planification, has been superceded by the pliable network in the morphology of social control. And so this object is available for recycling, ready for its former clarity to be transformed into a gridless, purposeless haze: "universal space", collapsed into an occupied blur of overlapping boundaries.

But the entropic blur should not be mistaken for an anti-grid, a liberation from the grids of power that regulate the modern city and more significantly, its outskirts. It is only the same grid, caught in the act of dissolution. Nor is there anything inherently liberating about the blurring of boundaries. Through reversals and repetitions of skins within skins, interwoven and collapsed together, this conjuncture of home and office yields no new syntheses – only zones of conflict and confusion. It is here, in these war zones, that negotiations regarding architecture's status are under way.

Transparency, iridescence, opacity, reflection and translucence are combined in an optical machine that intensifies, multiplies and interferes with programmed spatial relations in a flux of surface effects. Homeoffice is thus also cut adrift from its urban moorings. It is reduced to pure effect, a precisely delimited spatial sample that can be multiplied and arranged in any pattern desired, a pixel.

The interiors of this blur are inserted into an interactive system of images, and combined with other, comparable samples excerpted from mass culture. These include visual and written fragments of *Alphaville* (Jean-Luc Godard, 1965) and *The Trial* (Orson Welles, 1963), and segments of corporate advertising shorts and spreads from the same period celebrating new domestic and office technologies. This mediatic raw material, including the architecture, is dissolved into a series of interchangeable modulations.

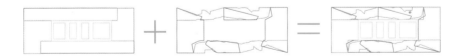

Grid

↓

Blur

Recycling

Are the old figures of domination empty enough to be melted down
and reused, shaped into new objects bearing new slogans? Invent nothing.
Recycle.

   Entropia's components are made from the ruins of modernity:
a 1960s office tower, a plastic suburban house, an abandoned embassy.
These become raw material for an architecture that makes no pretense
at *ex nihilo* innovation. It proceeds by identifying an object, reprocessing it,
and leaving it behind. Input/output. It remains indifferent to locale, leaping
from one carcass to the next. Its rule: locate every empty shell, every empty
container and empty it further. Do not refill. Only invert, or collapse. Each
entropic incident in turn exerts an influence beyond its own limits, since
it inevitably entails a dislocation, in which the object itself is uprooted
from its original locus and released into fluctuating distribution networks.
It disorganizes and reorganizes wherever it falls.

Homeoffice

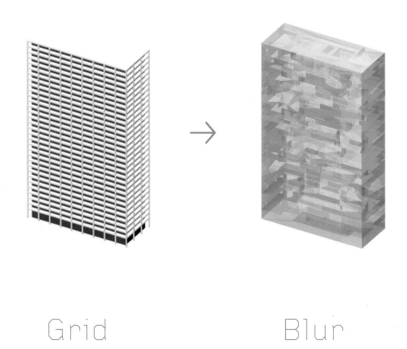

Grid → Blur

1

Reprogram the building into a half-and-half combination of residential and commercial
space: "home" and "office", zoned into two continuous volumes wrapping around one another.

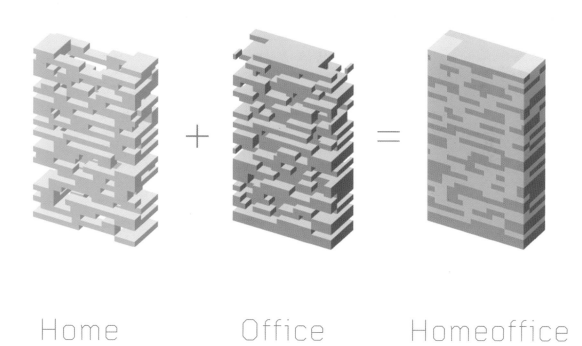

Home   +   Office   =   Homeoffice

2.

Clad "home" and "office" in transparent and semi-transparent glass skins, respectively.

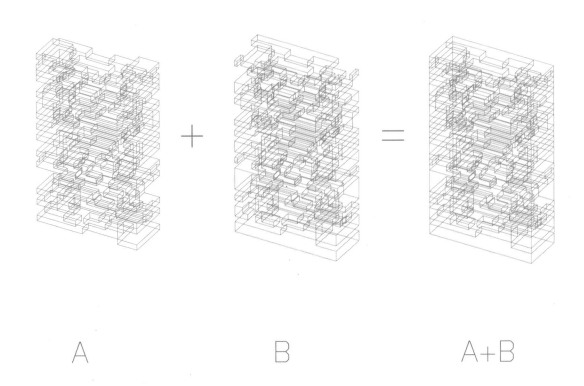

A   B   A+B

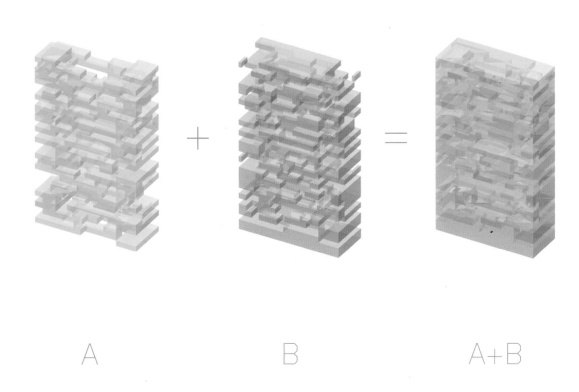

A　　　　　　　　B　　　　　　　A+B

3.

Duplicate the volume, reverse the skins ("home" = semi-transparent,
"office" = transparent), and implode the second set of skins.

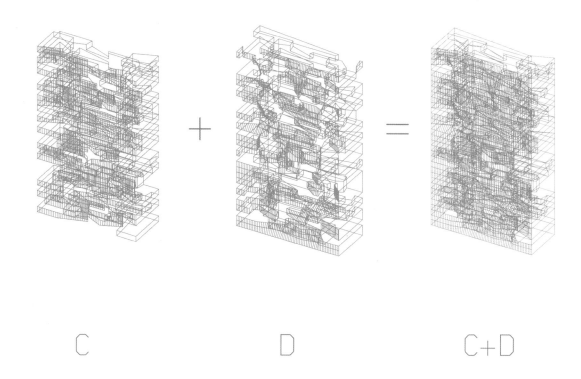

C   +   D   =   C+D

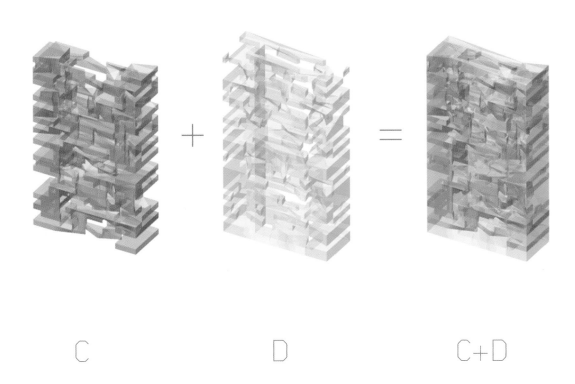

C   D   C+D

Combine all of the skins, producing a system of skins within skins. "Home" and "office" continuously rub up against one another, their boundaries intermingled as they become exposed and occluded on the corridor and on the street.

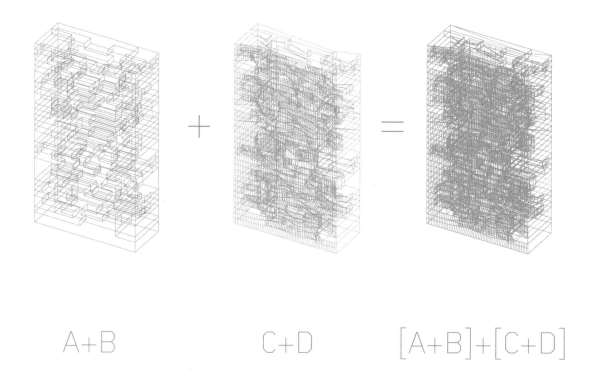

A+B   C+D   [A+B]+[C+D]

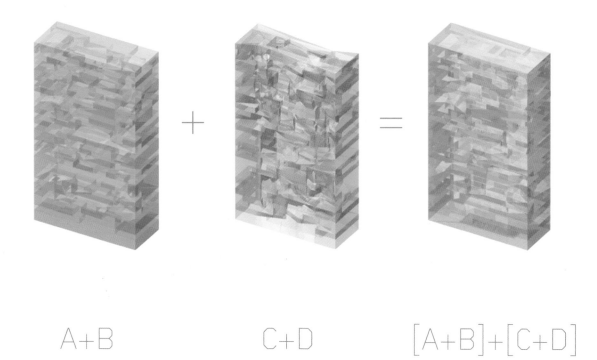

A+B   C+D   [A+B]+[C+D]

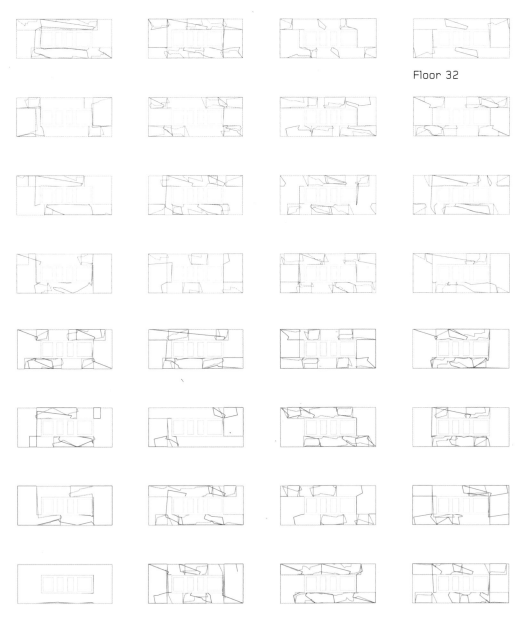

Floor 32

Floor 1

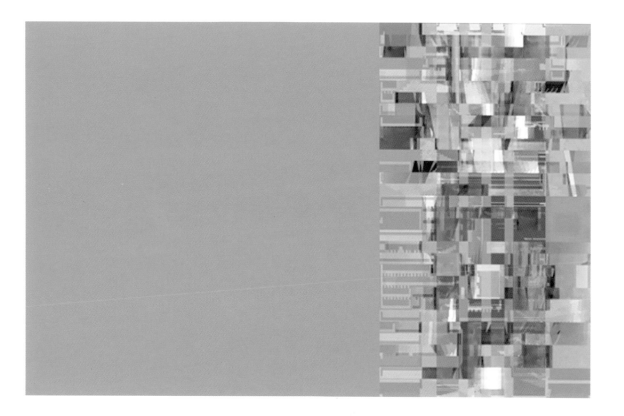

Exhibit A

Entropia cannot, by definition, be planned. Nor can it be avoided. It is, like its namesake, an irresistible tendency. The images presented in these pages are simply evidence entered into the official record, testimony as to its current status rather than a recipe for its manufacture. The failure in advance of every "visionary" architectural project is countered by the irrefutability of this evidence. Entropia is not a project. It merely occurs, irreversibly.

2

F03	A warm new American tradition in the making
F05	All over the US, gracious hosts & hostesses are discovering a new way of entertaining, that say to the guest "this is your home". Kitchen in the parlor!
F10	**Why? No one says "why", one says "because".**
F15	**Why? Because. Why? Because.**
F30	**You think more of what has been than of what will be.**
F31	**The past represents its future. It advances in a straight line, yet it ends by coming full circle.**
F32	**Yes! But in life one can know only the present.**
F37	**By the way things look, as well as the way they perform, our homes acquire new grace, new glamour, new accommodations, expressing not only the American love of beauty, but also the basic freedom of the American people, which is the freedom of individual choice.**
F46	**In life, all is linked, all is consequence.**

F37

F 1,3,15,25

"American Look", prod. Jam Handy Organization for General Motors Corporation (1958). Courtesy Prelinger Archives.

Interactive media sequence

Normalization
The loosening of the architectural object from its "grounds" – site, history, use, meaning – represents a counterstrategy to each and every desperate effort to authorize its existence. Entropia remains illegitimate, unauthorized. It is a code violation, not because it flaunts architectural or urbanistic convention, but because it acknowledges the conventionality of officially sanctioned deviance. It is perfectly normal.

F 37,46

Interactive media sequence

3

F04	I wish, I wish the faucet wouldn't drip all day I wish the refrigerator door will close and stay closed I wish I had a stove whose pilot light was always lit Furthermore, A kitchen phone in hand when friends call to chat a bit Hello, yes, this is Mary, how are you, bye They say your kitchen dazzles every eye A brand new sink, a built-in oven A new refrigerator and a phone A kitchen phone, a bright red phone Got to go, good bye, good bye, good bye, I'll call you later.
F06	**I see, people have become slaves of possibilities.**

F04

F11	Exactly what am I charged with?
F12	**You think the future is a fact. Isn't it?**
F14	**Everything has been said provided words do not change their meaning, and meanings their words.**

F21	Muzak helps solve "people problems"
F22	Proof
F24	Even your best employees will often seek escape from tension, monotony, fatigue or noise. And so you suffer from lateness, extended coffee breaks or lunch hours, early departures.
F25	Cut these losses with scientifically planned work music by Muzak. It helps create a pleasantly stimulating work environment. Your people work better, are less prone to errors, accidents, lateness and time wasting.

F 04,21,30

F04

Interactive media sequence

"Once Upon a Honeymoon", prod. Jerry Fairbanks Productions for the Bell System (1956). Courtesy Prelinger Archives.

From-to

From this to that. Hardly an index of "things as they really were"
or will be, the from-to story is more likely to be evidence of things
"as advertised". Entropia both requires and redistributes such progressions.
From SOM to Homeoffice. From Formica to Open House. From US embassy
to.... Within each is a gap, since the source material represents neither
an historical ground from which the future is extrapolated, nor a fully
knowable or containable past from which the future deviates. It merely
repeats, in another form.

And so repetition, that heroically modern figuration of the commodity
form, is recycled as a weapon against the from-to story. It is not that the
history of space, registered in stories about its consumption (from real
estate to signspace), is moving in the wrong direction. It is that it appears
to be moving at all. The from-to story – describing the inexorable advance
of the commodity form into every architectural crevice (from this
architecture to that architecture) – is the very figure of consumption itself:
Dynamic obsolescence of spatial models. Against this figure we deploy our
repetitions, like small, cryptic signals, the oscillations of which gradually
increase in frequency until all is a steady, intolerable hum. That is history.

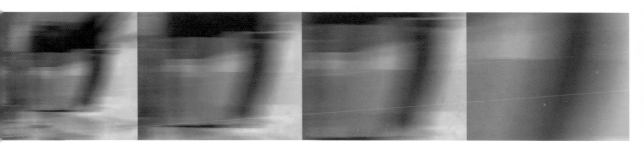

.com

The components of Entropia all tend in some way toward uselessness.
Which is to say that their apparent functionality is interfered with by the
mutations they undergo. In that sense, they aspire to the highest form of
instrumentality: sublime indifference. Hardly negative, this uselessness
can be shown to represent a maximum of stored potential. Its only
weakness lies in its inability to outpace the markets, in which
indeterminate, future value.com remains considerably more attractive
than demonstrable productivity. Even Entropia is not useless enough.

F 42+

Interactive media sequence

4

F15	What's that up there?
	The computer.
F18	One of those electronic gimmicks? They give you the answer to anything?
F19	**The task of Alpha60 is to calculate and project.**
F40	From our work has come breakthrough after breakthrough in science providing the intricate devices that lie at the heart of the telephone service of tomorrow. Through the invention of better things, we are trying very hard to give you the kind of telephone service you want and need. And we think you will agree, after seeing the many exhibits we have here, that there is no end to telephone progress now, or in century twenty one.
F41	**I shall calculate so that the future is impossible.**
F55	Playmate... Make a date with the Playmate, take it anywhere.
F56	Smart sculptured beauty that makes the Playmate perfect for the bedroom, kitchen, den, anywhere!
F57	Take it anywhere.
F60	Uncanny. Uncomplicated. Uncommon.
F61	Language controlled. Functional modularity.
F62	Superfast.

Yesterday

What is the future of architecture? An irrelevant question, since it
assumes an organic link to evolutionary time. In its place we can ask:
What new topologies of past, present, and future can be engineered?
Here modernism's engineer returns as an architectural agent after
almost a century of rest, now sitting at a lab bench and surrounded by
microprocessors. This engineer-turned-lab technician is today more than
ever responsible for the production of a "natural" history. Evolution takes
place in the laboratory, and life itself is patented. Under these conditions,
architecture has been relocated from its formerly heroic position as herald
of a new age and refunctioned simultaneously as inert background and
hysterical image, both of which represent stages in a tendency toward
entropy. Neutrality or overload. Boxes or Bilbao. There is little difference.

5

F05   Women and men alike are increasingly interested in the look of things. They eagerly give their attention to what is new, beautiful and advanced. Modern packaging does more than wrap and hold and conceal, stunning in color, ingenious in design, it brings festivities to the market-place, tempting, hinting and revealing.

F07   We are unique, dreadfully unique. The meaning of words and of expressions is no longer grasped. An isolated word, or a detail of a design can be understood, but the meaning of the whole escapes.

F26   Once we know the number one, we believe that we know the number two, because one plus one equals two. We forget that first we must know the meaning of "plus".

F27   Time is like a circle which turns endlessly.
       The arc that climbs is the future. The descending arc is the past.

F28   This is a copying machine and this is a good question. Why did Xerox build the 813 copier when every well regulated office already has a copying machine? The things you need to make copies here are simple enough – ordinary papers, ordinary carbons, ordinary erasers, ordinary cards, and an extraordinary someone to put these things together.

F32   Everything matches, even the letter trays.
F33   In all colors.

F 01,05,15,32
F 25, 26

F37

F28

Interactive
media sequence

"American Look", prod. Jam Handy Organization for General Motors Corporation (1958), courtesy Prelinger Archives.

"The 813 & Why", prod. Jam Handy Organization for the Xerox Corporation (1963). Courtesy Prelinger Archives.

30

The wall

The dystopia of a world without borders looms as an outer limit for architectural and urbanistic speculation. Entropia responds with a complex of tightly bounded spatial units. If the outside is inside, freedom can no longer be simply a question of tearing down walls, if indeed it ever was. Instead, we are given a new set of thresholds, breached and re-formed through a series of topological transformations. Things within things, and within themselves, are turned inside-out, upside down. And tearing down walls only leads to further spatial complications: the more open things are, the more closed they are.

In Entropia, domestic interiors reconfigure urban agglomerations, and underground bunkers redraw the maps of power above. The compulsion to aggregate is confronted with an unbearable dispersion, where nothing is connected to anything and screens glow with an artificiality comparable only to that of the lights glaring over a parking lot. The city after the metropolis – this is the space of Entropia.

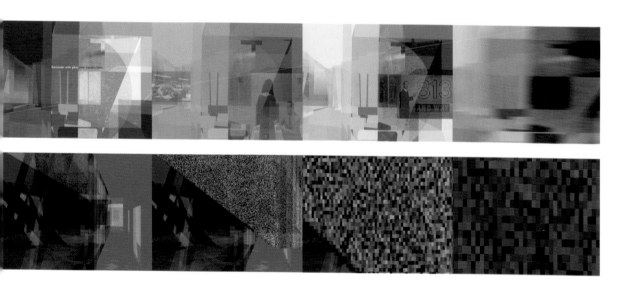

F 27,28,30,31,
F 32,33,34+

Interactive media sequence

Value added

"But Celebration is not alone in the greater Orlando area in capitalizing on an attractive commercial downtown core to complement and stimulate residential development. The central cores are helping to sell houses to buyers from afar, coming to a region that has gained an international profile, and a large new employment base, through its recreational attractions." (*The New York Times*, "Around Orlando, A Sharper Focus on Downtowns," Real Estate, Sunday, 12 December, 1999, 1).

And:

"In the years to come, a globalized Internet economy may allow some of us to re-root ourselves by freeing us from centralized workplaces. It has already begun to do so. But the electronic e-topia of the Internet, no matter how sophisticated it becomes, offers no real alternative to the values arising from a strong sense of place." (*The New York Times*, "The Allure of Place in a Mobile World", editorial, Wednesday, 15 December, 1999, A22.)

Thus the selling of place, a process always already under way in all deterritorializations. This is place as corporate commodity, value-added in the form of innumerable downtown cultural centers and main streets to make emptiness more palatable. And thus also its cliché-ridden complement, the net, spins its subjects into a resurgent modern, isotropic "universal space". It is an old story. "The values arising from a strong sense of place." Gingerbread, laced with venom.

F 56

Interactive media sequence

LMvdR

Entropia is haunted by the ghosts of Mies (three blind Mies). Impossible, multiplicitous space lodged within, or below, the inert neutrality of the box. Homeoffice: The second glass skyscraper, shattered and caught in a skin-only homage to Seagram. Open House: The courtyard house with automobile, inverted to capture its suburban prey. Embassy: The modular scrambling of remote power gone underground, following the tentative lead of the unrealized consulate in São Paolo and even more, that of the official, empty embassy of architecture itself, Crown Hall.

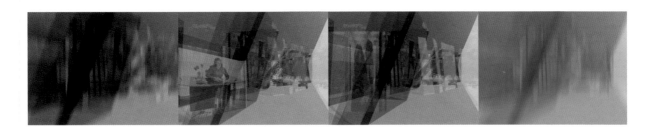

6

F05	How to handle women?
F25	What should men do when a woman cries? Are women logical? A woman answers for the benefit of men bosses.
F30	Doctors are now prescribing an ataraxic medicine. It makes those who fear they are about to quit feel like they are ready to begin, bidding their darkened spirits goodbye, for the calming peace of a cloudless sky. Of all the states throughout this nation, the happiest by far is the state of relaxation. There will be fewer breakdowns and insomniacs when more of us have learned to be relaxed. We will be free to relish the joys of freedom.
F37	It has been said that the logic of this story is a dream, a nightmare.
F56	This door was intended for you, only for you. And now, I am going to close it.

F 15

F 01,05,29,34

"The Relaxed Wife", prod. On Film for J. B. Roerig and Co., 1957 Courtesy Prelinger Archives.

Interactive media sequence

Signal

↓

Noise

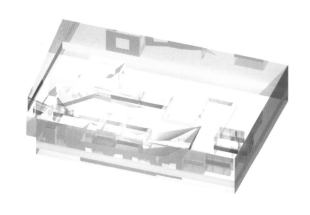

Formica Corporation World's Fair House, sample
sheet, 1964. Courtesy Formica Corporation.

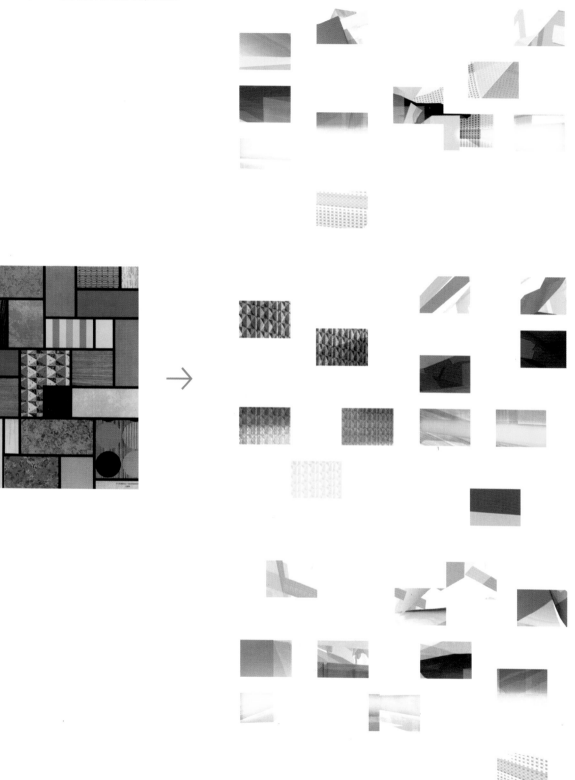

Open House

Circles, or Things that diagram their diagrams

The cul-de-sac as allegory – history turning in on itself, going around and around. When this inversion is itself inverted, history spins off into limitless tangents. Serpentine demarcation lines, or inside-out cul-de-sacs, serve to maximize both isolation and exposure (formerly "frontage") for the new open houses. Front and back no longer apply. The backyard, or the unconscious of the lawn, is erased, thus upsetting the balance and unleashing the full force of an unmanageable desire to contain the complete circumference of the house in a single, unified field. The preferred mowing pattern now proceeds in circles or, in the most extreme cases, not at all.

FORMICA CORPORATION

Inside-out cul-de-sacs

Formica World Fair House, Emil Schmidlin, architect. Queens New York, 1964.
Formica® logo. Courtesy Formica Corporation.

39

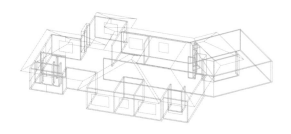

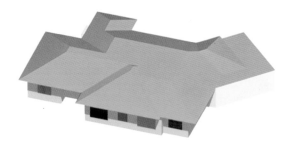

1.

Take a 1960s suburban ranch house.

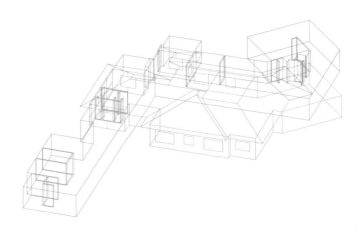

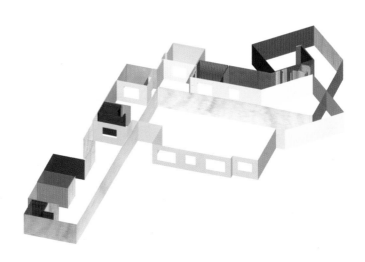

2.

Detach its inner surfaces.

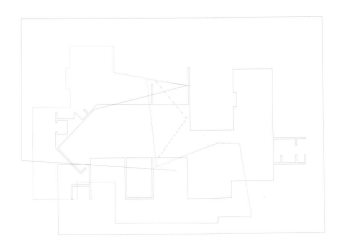

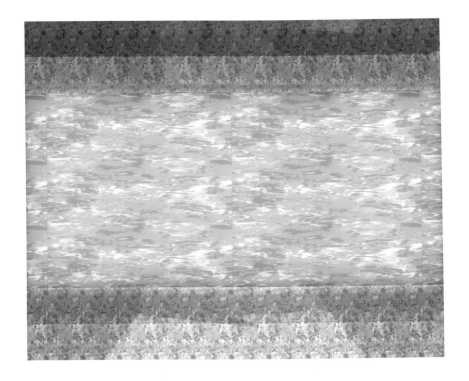

Detail   Plan

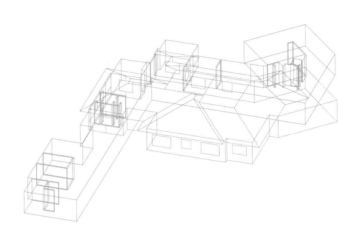

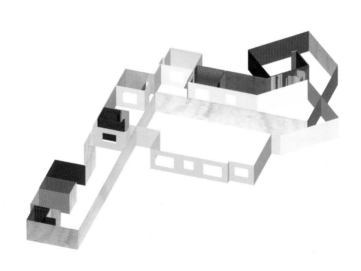

2.

Detach its inner surfaces.

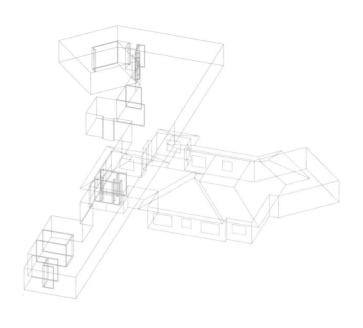

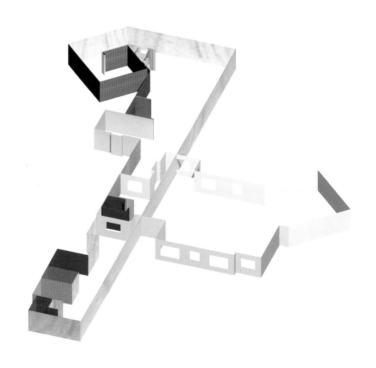

3.

Turn the inner surfaces inside-out.

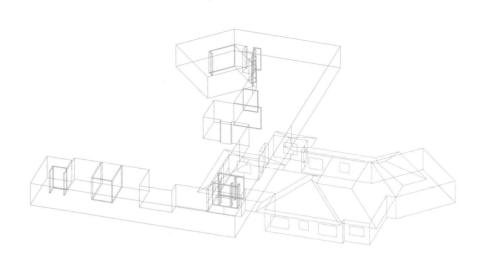

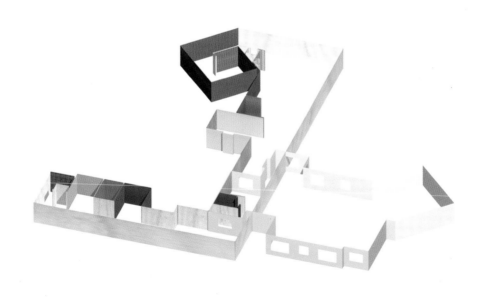

4

Keep turning...

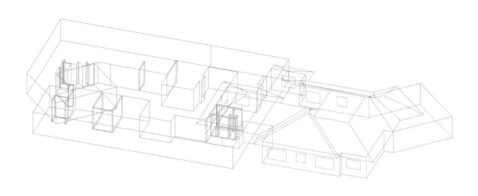

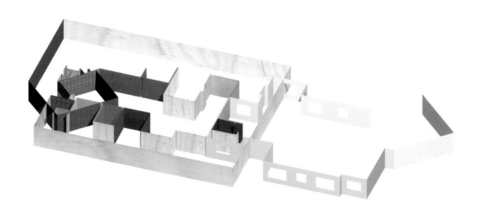

...until a courtyard house is formed.

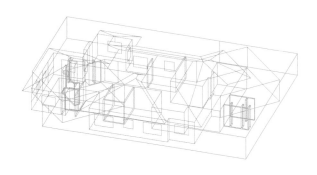

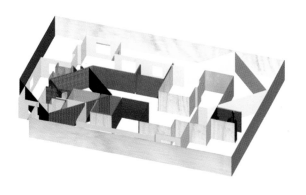

6

Embed the ranch house (the outer skin) in the courtyard house (the inner skin).

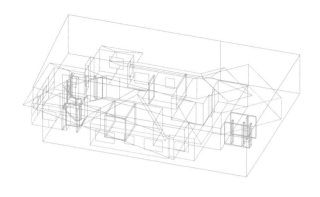

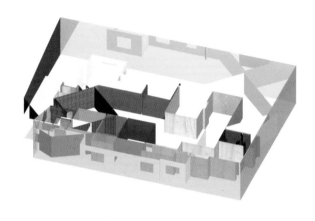

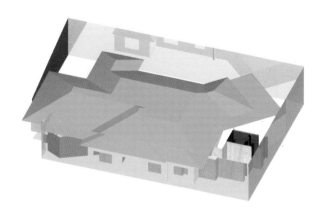

7

Twist the inner and outer skin (plus roof) of the garage back together into the center of the house, pulling them inside-out (again) below the main volume. Convert the outer wall (formerly the wall dividing the hallway in two) into a one-way mirror facing inwards (you can see in, they cannot see out).

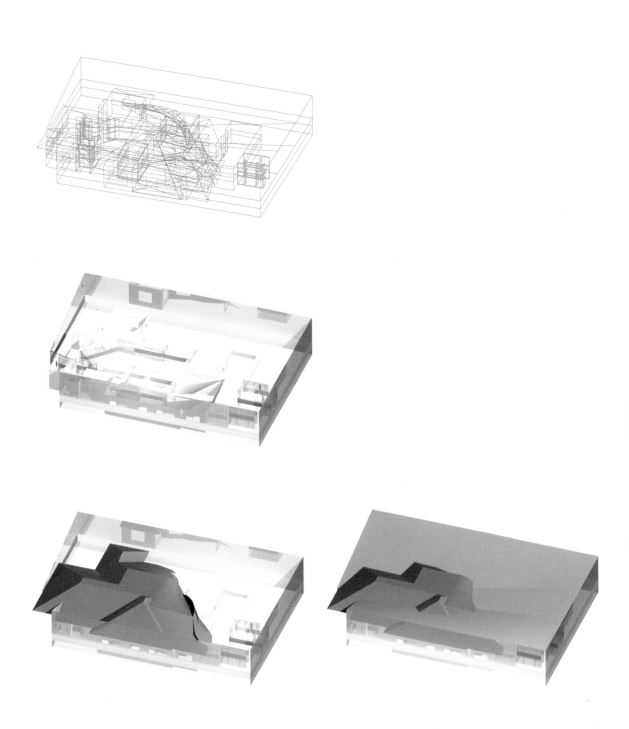

8.

Convert the color-coded interior surfaces to black and white, with degrees
of transparency indexed to tone, and cover the box with a mirrored ceiling.

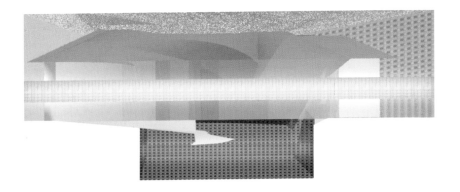

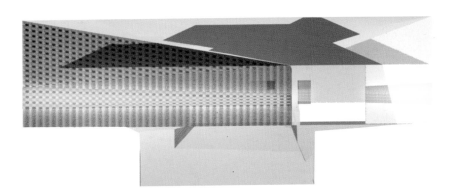

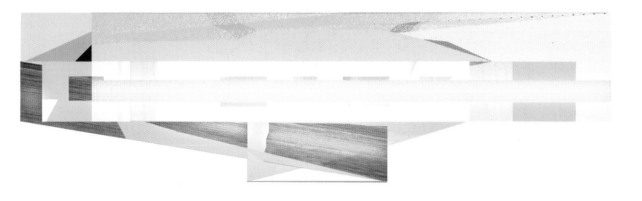

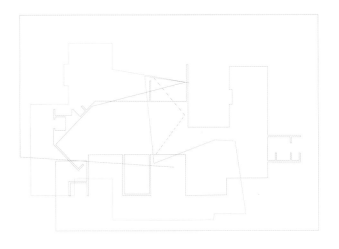

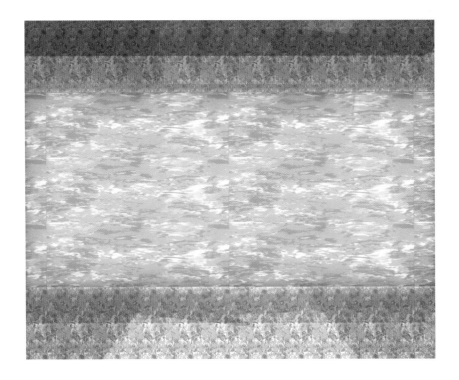

Detail | Plan

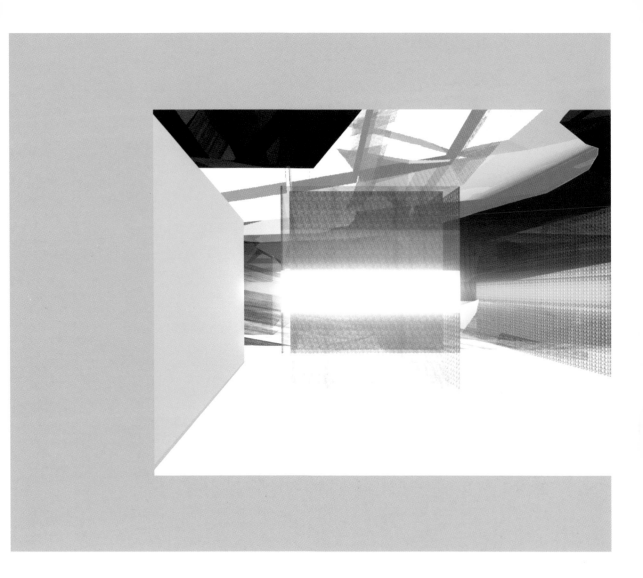

Bliss

Entropia manifests an urbanity-degree-zero that recovers the estrangements and dislocations squeezed out of the metropolis in altered form. The process begins with disaffection and ends with an exhilarating indifference to the sanitized social whole. The city is not an organism, wherever it is, whatever form it takes. This is the lesson of the highway interchange, the strip mall, the office park. This new urbanity trembles with overtones even more sinister than those that haunted its modern predecessor. Bourgeois intolerance has become "family values". But the hardened, smiling sheen of suburban bliss is always stained with the actualities of disaggregation, like the pockmarked face of a shy teenager.

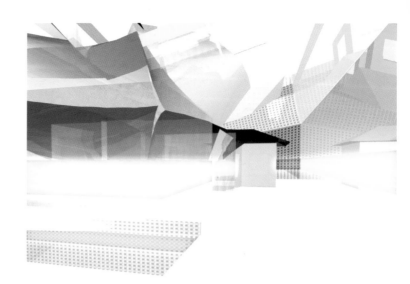

First of all, daughter has changed from school clothes to something more festive. Dressing a little makes her feel, and consequently *look*, more charming. Even the table takes on a special air.

Can you *look* through the glass? Can you see me now?

Looks **and feels like wood but is largely *plastic* laminate.**

I just want to say one word to you, just one word.

Yes sir.

Are you listening?

Yes sir, I am.

Plastics.

Exactly how do you mean?

There is a great *future* in plastics. Think about it, will you think about it?

Yes, I will.

Enough said, that's a deal.

Advanced **but not *futuristic*.**

Contemporary communication also means knowledge and culture; and each technical *advance means* that we have more of each, for more levels of our population.

I have got this feeling ever since I graduated, it's a kind of compulsion where I have to be rude all the *time*, you know what I *mean*? Like I am playing some kind of a game, but the rules don't make sense to me. They are being made by all the other people. No, I mean, no one makes them up – they seem to make themselves up.

They don't pick this *time* of the day to spring unpleasant surprises on Dad. If they have disagreeable news, they will postpone the discussion until another time. And this is no time to bother Dad for a raise in your allowance, new clothes or to argue about other financial matters. Ah! dinner time...

Mother, too changes form her daytime clothes. The women in this family seem to feel that they owe it to the men of the family to look *relaxed*, rested and attractive at dinnertime.

Contemporary mode of *relaxed* informality is heightened by no *worry* materials.

Hey, what's the matter?

Dad, could you explain to them that I have to be alone for awhile.

I am just...

Worried?

Well, I guess about my future...

What about it?

I don't know, I want it to be...

To be what?

Different.

The word contemporary is so much a part of our language nowadays that it would seem almost unnecessary to define it. We distinguish it subtly from the word "modern" which implies a complete break with the past. And we distinguish it also from *modern* but *different* ideas of nations & cultures.

How about art?

Art, that's a good subject. You start it off.

I don't know anything about it.

Well, what do you want to know? Are you interested more in *modern* art or classical art?

Neither.

Then why did you ask about it?

You wanted to have a *conversation*.

Brother seats junior, then helps mother to her chair as he would his best girl. Well, the dinner date has begun, and they are all happy about it. Napkins on the lap, the family awaits service. They converse pleasantly while Dad serves. I said pleasantly, for that is the keynote at dinnertime. It is not only good manners but good sense. Pleasant, unemotional *conversation* helps digestion.

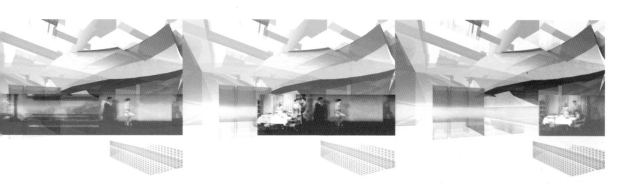

"A Date with Your Family", Edward C. Simmel, 1950. Courtesy Prelinger Archives.

Interactive media sequence

"A Date with Your Family",
Edward C. Simmel, 1950
Courtesy Prelinger Archives

Formica, World's Fair House, 1964. Interiors
Courtesy Formica Corporation

Interactive media sequence

These boys greet their Dad as though they are genuinely glad to see him, as though they have really missed being away from him during the day, and they are anxious to talk to him. This is the time for *pleasant* discussion in a thoroughly relaxed mood.

Fair *House* is middle of the road design aimed at *pleasing* a mass market.

For God's sake, Mrs. Robinson, here we are, you got me into your *house*, you give me a drink, you put on music, you start opening your personal life to me and telling me your husband won't be back for hours, and I would say you are trying to seduce me.

Make your new house say "open *house*" with Acrylite building products.

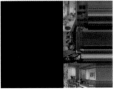

Let father and mother guide the conversational trends as they desire, after all they *make* all this possible, and they may want to talk over their day with each other. Tell mother how good the food is, and maybe sis rates a *compliment* too. It makes them want to continue pleasing you.

Blue tones are cool; red are hot. *Complimentary* but not contrasting colors may be combined. *Dark* colors make objects look smaller than light colors.

Will you come in please?

What?

I'd like you to come in till I get the lights on.

Would you mind walking ahead of me till the sun porch? I *feel* funny coming into a *dark* house.

But there is light there.

Please.

What do you drink? Bourbon?

Look, Mrs. Robinson, I drove you home, I was glad to do it, but I have some things on my mind. Can you understand that?

Dressing a little makes her *feel* and consequently look more charming. Even the table takes on a special air. Mother too changes from her daytime clothes. The women in this family seem to feel that they owe it to the men of the family to look relaxed, rested and attractive at dinnertime.

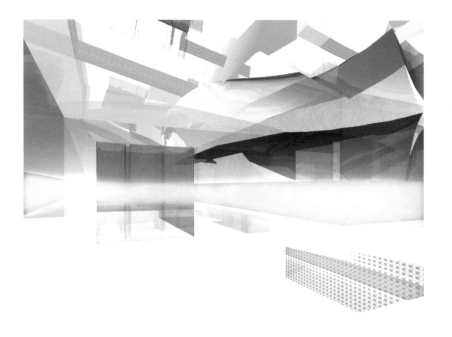

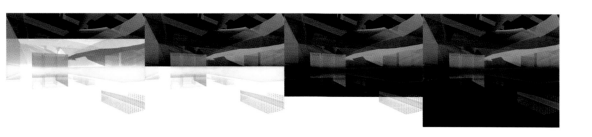

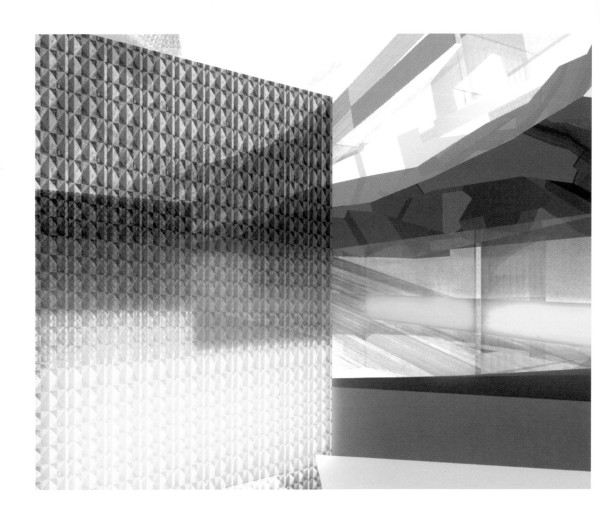

A *Kitchen* that is in love with my wife.
A messy *kitchen*. It's beautiful, it's beautiful.
Formica® – on walls, on doors, on *kitchen* cabinets, on window sills,
on the furniture, as bathtub enclosure, even on *door* knobs.
We don't have to even lock the *doors* in Stepford, that is really
something, isn't it?
Why can't you just lock the *door* and go to bed? I am pretty neurotic.
Please wait till my husband gets back.

When is he *coming* back?
It *comes* with the house, part of the deal.
Everything in her house looked like a *TV* commercial.
All may be dimmed for *TV*.
Maybe, I thought, I will put the pool table over here.
Conceding that few consumers *may* be ready for plastic-laminate
housing, Lefferts nevertheless predicts the house will open a lot
of eyes.

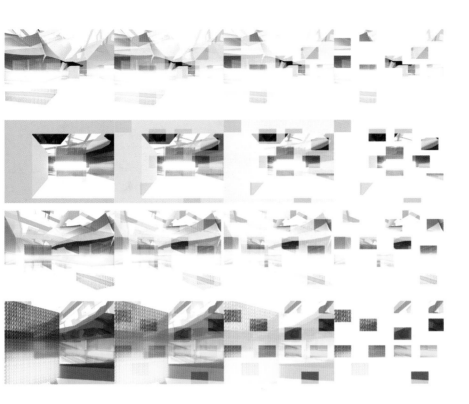

Vision

Unlike the revolution, Entropia is and will continue to be televised. Its coordinates are given by all of the possible combinations of numbers on your remote. It penetrates your deepest interior in the form of an uncontrollably live feed pouring out of the screen. Its slogan: There is nothing more real than an image.

If Entropia can also be said to be interactive, it is only because interaction is offered as a last resort, the only means of producing a momentary interruption in the relentless monotony of its repetitions. Point and click. Like changing the channels, such interruptions only underscore the interchangeability of its contents, by ushering in more of the same. This interchangeability, evidenced by the unexpected repetition of something you just saw, something that was on last week, elicits a familiar disorientation. This is the disorientation of always being in the same place, wherever you are. Wherever you go, there you are.

Entropia, therefore, stands poised on the threshold between intense differentiation and utter sameness. Both roads lead to entropy, and along each are to be found profuse opportunities for both escape and compliance. The escape routes do not lead outside of this differentiated indifference but further in; thus, the intensified scrambling of insides and outsides is the Entropian *modus operandi*. And if the only way out is in, that is because Entropia is founded on the unstable ground of an empty interior. The fact that there's nothing inside offers immense hope.

Interactive media sequence

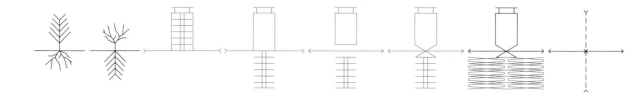

Embassy

The United States embassy in Saigon (now Ho Chi Minh City), Vietnam, designed by the firm of Curtis & Davis and opened in 1967, was recently demolished to make way for the new world order it helped to usher in. Entropia harbors its ghost. The original, raised from the dead, is a gridded, concrete volume containing six floors of rudimentary modular offices (cells) along a double-loaded central corridor. This assembly is wrapped in a cynical *brise-soleil* screen, late of Edward Durrell Stone in New Delhi. The entire compound is surrounded by a wall at the street edge: a territory within a territory. There is a helipad on the roof.

In the new version, deprived of their pretensions to military-industrial paternalism with the departure of the last helicopter in the 1975 evacuation, the inner cells go underground, upside down, leaving behind an empty box above. The first floor, previously "welcoming" and now just below the ground plane, becomes unnecessary and is removed, leaving behind only elevators and stairwells. Entrance is displaced from horizontal to vertical, becoming purely a matter of descent and rendering the street wall redundant.

The inner (hallway side) walls of each office are shrunk down to become two-sided electronic screens, suspended in the original outline of the office at eye level. These are doubled and projected, along with the trace outline of the former offices, to the outer perimeter. The space of each cell is thus stretched out into an attenuated, diminishing volume that terminates in a two-sided screen at the outer perimeter and doubles back on itself in an identical volume terminating in a two-sided screen along the hallway. The box above, utterly empty, is colored black in recognition of a new, electronic regime in which the corporation is indistinguishable from the state, and equipped with a glowing Entropian logo. It is an embassy without a territory, one that can only interface with, and spy on, itself.

The only space accessible from above is the hallway, now lined with impenetrable screens projected inward from the outer edges of the former embassy compound, and vice versa – screens staring outward at nothing. The stretched out, washed out space of the former office cells is accessed only remotely (that is, as an image), just as it is in this book. On the screens runs continuous surveillance footage of Entropia: open houses, homeoffices and embassies, seen from inside-out – the same images you see in the pages of this book. You look in, with the help of an image-machine (a book/screen/building), only to discover that this machine is only ever scanning its own images in an infinite repeat-loop. Neither autonomous zone nor think tank, this empty bunker – harboring only glowing, flickering images – is a space of sensory deprivation that reorganizes the territorialities of state and corporate power into an underground implosion.

Likewise its interiors, which are – in the end – only images of other images, are combined with cinematic images of paranoid, underground spaces from *THX 1138* (George Lucas, 1970) and *The Andromeda Strain* (Robert Wise, 1971), along with news coverage of the Vietnam War. These are reformatted, remixed, and recirculated via interactive digital sequences organized into a grid of security monitors that cascades, upon closer inspection, into more of the same. The millions of colors of entropic light that illuminate both the spaces and their screens add up, ultimately, to zero. Breakdown.

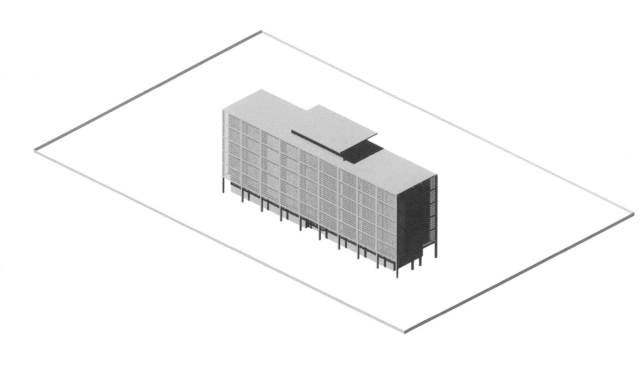

Cell

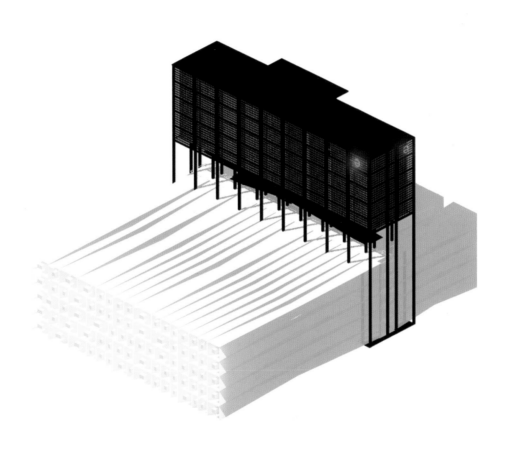

→ Screen

United States embassy, Saigon. Curtis & Davis, 1967.

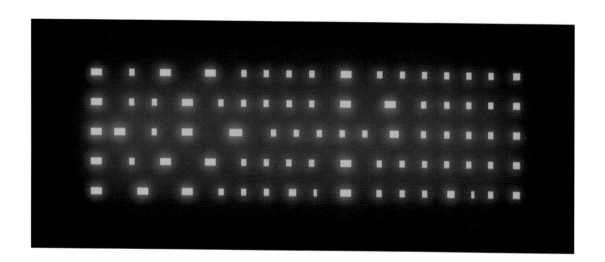

Skins

The surface of things, to which Entropia is dedicated, represents a primary site of contestation over where you want to go today. It is the future, literally, as advertised. Are you ready? It is the vehicle of brand loyalty and medium of identification with the corporate image. Here one and only one stratagem is deployed: dissolution. Dissolve the skin, wash it out, scramble its codes. Remember that the outside is everywhere – inside the house, underground, behind glass. Do not attempt to look for "deeper meanings". Instead, empty the logo further. Invert it, collapse it.

Embassy, underground elevation

Metamorphosis
Looking into the mirror upon awakening, architecture no longer recognized itself.

.org

There is nothing organic about Entropia. Its flatness, its coldness, and its emptiness dry out the organs, infrastructures, and systems of modernity. In their place it leaves phantoms: ghostly organizations, shadowy networks, hallucinatory wholes. They are there if you look.

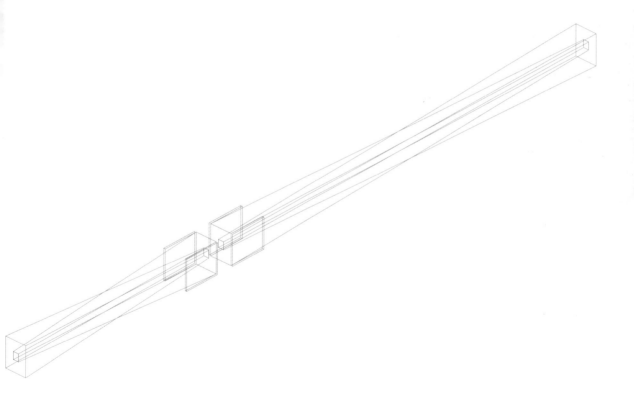

Cell-to-screen, detail

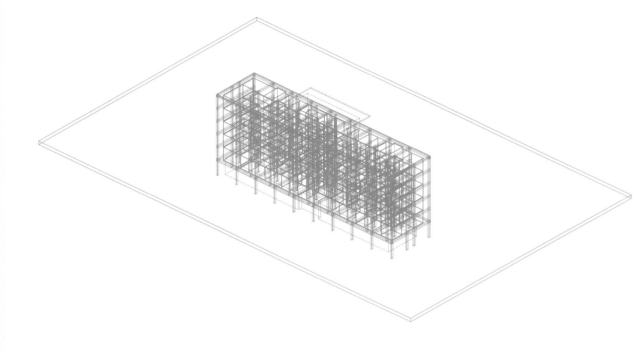

1.

Reconstruct the original embassy.

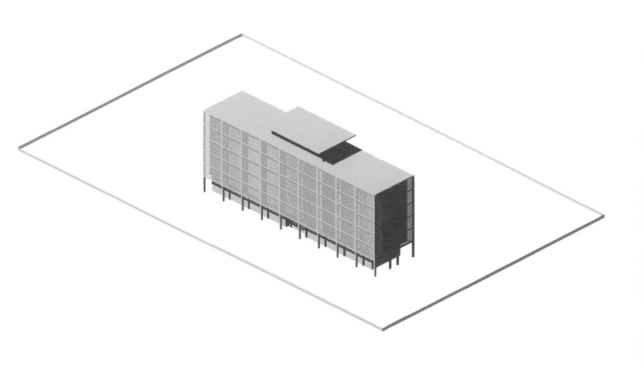

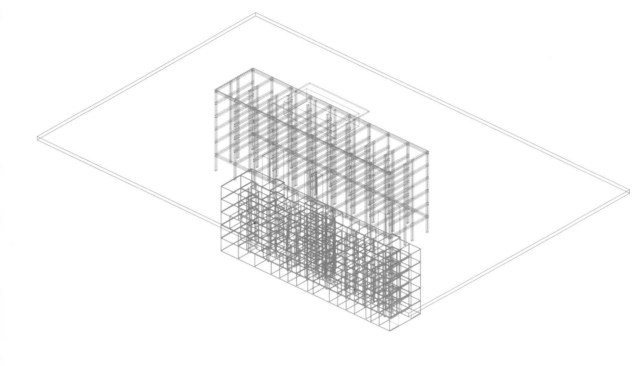

2.

Pull its office-cells underground, leaving an empty shell above.

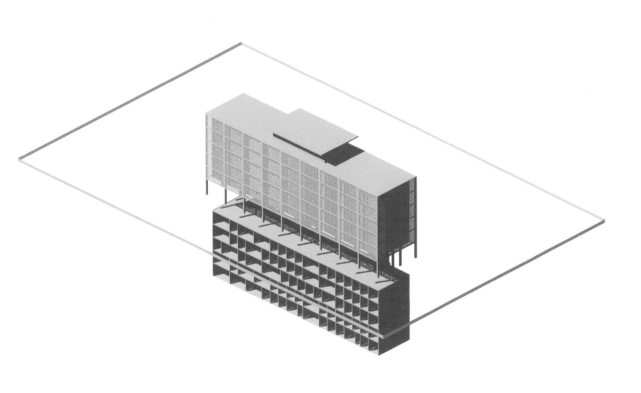

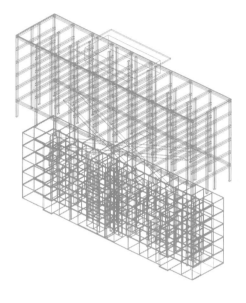

3.

Twist the upside-down cells to reorient "front" to "back" and vice versa. The
infrastructure twists with them. The street wall, now superfluous, disappears.

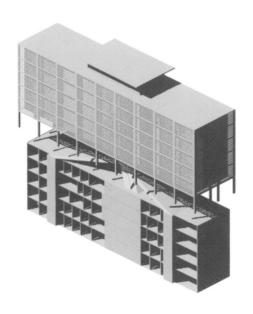

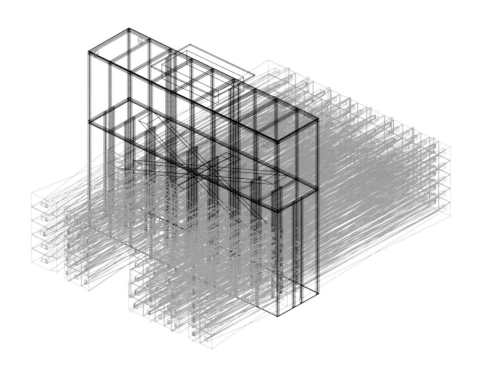

4

Shrink the inner (hallway side) surfaces of each office down to become two-sided electronic
screens, suspended at eye level. Double them and project them, along with the trace outline
of the former offices, to the outer perimeter. Color the box black. Add logo.

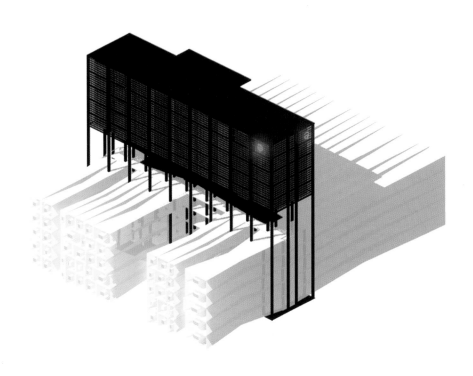

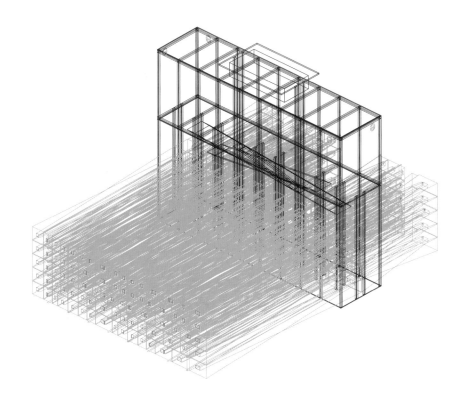

5.

Look at the machine, a machine designed to look at itself.

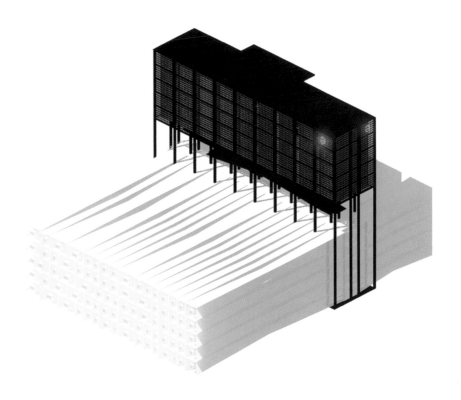

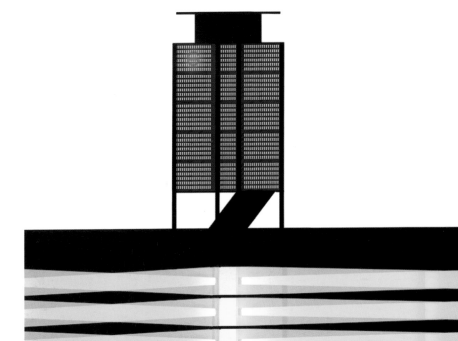

Longitudinal section

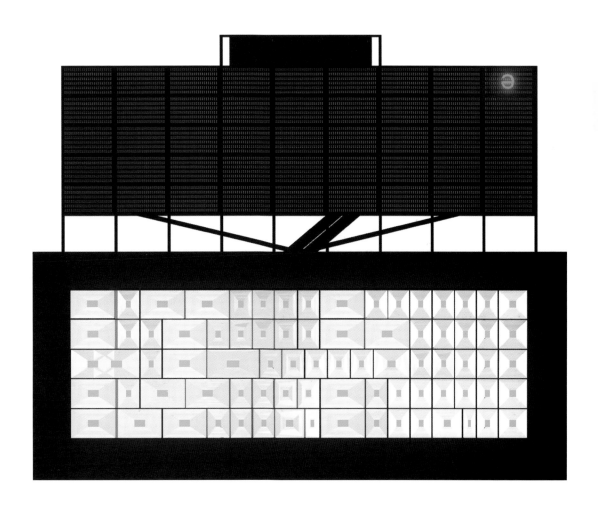

Lateral section

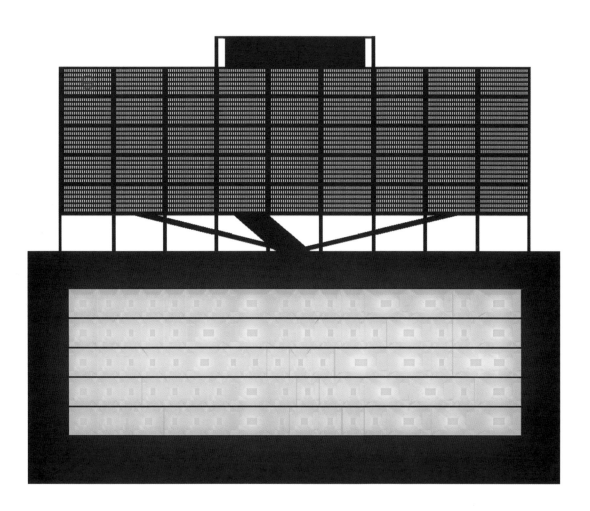

Lateral section at hallway

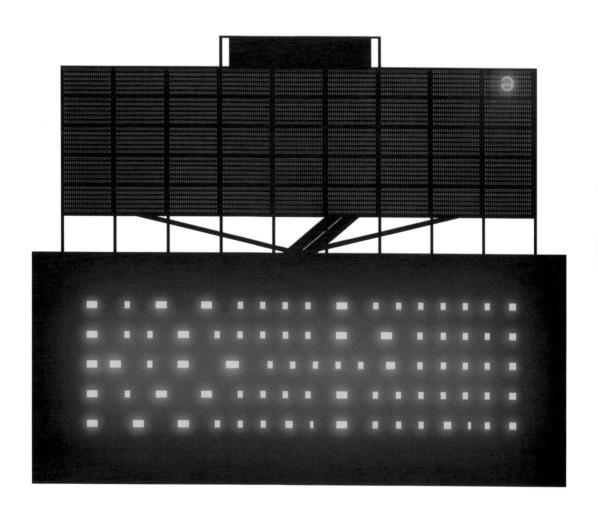

Elevation

RGB

Entropia is pixellated. Its eversions follow a chromatopology in which space is at the mercy of color-coding and scale is replaced by resolution. Its anamorphoses accelerate the cryptological inevitability of an entropic loss of information. Each decoding is followed by a recoding, which is necessarily accompanied by an incremental increase in interference.

Entropia's colors are in turn inseparable from the light of the screen in all its forms. Each of its components is calibrated to maximize the effect of this luminosity, and in so doing, to lay claim on its irreducible artificiality. Entropia's optics – its transparencies, its translucence, its reflections, its refractions, its glow – are therefore synchronized with its degenerative logistics.

Black box, interior

31 January 1968

A 17-man Vietcong squad seized parts of the United States Embassy in the center of Saigon and held them for six hours early today.

The Vietcong, wearing South Vietnamese Army uniforms, held off American policemen firing machine guns and rocket launchers. Finally, the invaders were routed by squads of American paratroopers who landed by helicopter on the roof of the building.

(Buckley, Tom. "Foe Invades U.S. Saigon Embassy; Raiders Wiped Out After 6 Hours; Vietcong Widen Attack on Cities", *The New York Times*, 31 January 1968).

30 April 1975

The United States exit from South Vietnam, like so much that preceded it, was dictated by events in Saigon that outpaced hopes in Washington.

President Ford ordered the evacuation of the last remnants of the American presence – the United States Embassy in Saigon and the defense attache's compound at nearby Tan Son Nhut airport – after Ambassador Graham A. Martin reluctantly recommended, at 10:41 o'clock last night, "We should go with Option 4".

Option 4 was the plan for the immediate evacuation by helicopter of all remaining American citizens and as many South Vietnamese as possible.

(Naughton, James, M. "Call For Pullout, Then a Night's Vigil at White House", *The New York Times*, 30 April 1975).

1 May 1975

"It is our embassy now", said a laughing young Vietnamese soldier as he pranced gleefully along the littered hallway of the administrative building.

The handsome embassy building on Thong Nhut Boulevard was abandoned by a detachment of United States marines at 7:50 this morning. They remained behind after Ambassador Graham A. Martin left, to prevent waiting Vietnamese from rushing the last helicopters.

(Arnett, Peter. "Looters Rush the Abandoned U.S. Embassy in Saigon," *The New York Times*, 1 May 1975).

1 May 1975

Another memento from the embassy that was saved was a color portrait of former President Richard M. Nixon and his family, inscribed "To Ambassador and Mrs. Graham Martin with appreciation for their service to the nation. From Richard Nixon".

A French businessman who said he was taking refuge in the New Zealand Embassy grabbed the picture.

"I know the ambassador", he said. "I will personally deliver it to him in the United States some time in the future".

Outside the embassy, Thong Nhut Boulevard was littered with burned cars.

(Esper, George. "Communists Take Over Saigon; U.S. Rescue Fleet Is Picking Up Vietnamese Who Fled in Boats", *The New York Times*, 1 May 1975).

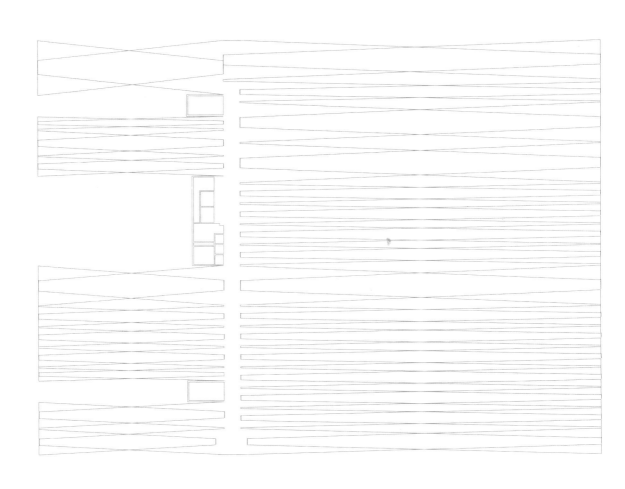

Plan, below grade

Hallway interior

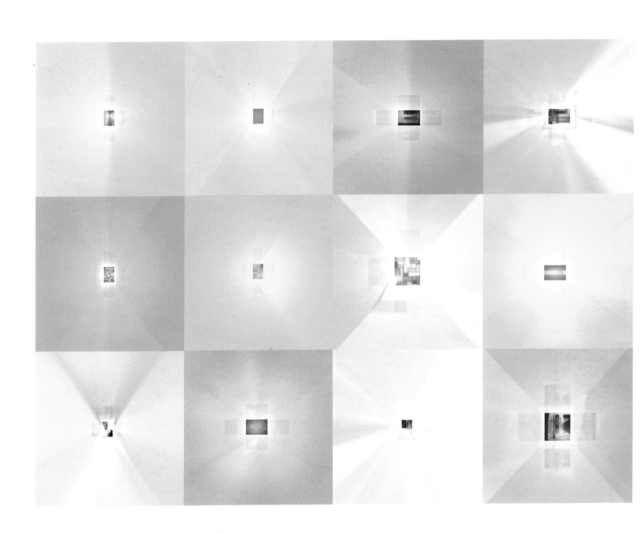

Interactive media sequence

What's wrong? Never mind. Could you be more specific? *This is an open transmission.* There's nothing left to say about this war, there's just nothing left to say. If you have a problem, don't hesitate to ask for assistance. *It should have been left to the scientist. It's a colossal mistake. Tell the president I said so.* North Vietnam cannot defeat or humiliate the United States. Only Americans can do that. Thank you for being conscientious. A visual record is being taken and filed with the department of biological flow. *I never liked red lights.* But let men everywhere know, however, that a strong, and a confident and a vigilant America stands ready tonight to seek an honorable peace – and stands ready tonight to defend an honored cause – whatever the price, whatever the burden, whatever the sacrifice that duty may require. Back off THX 1138, back off for a second. Take four capsules; in ten minutes take two more. If you feel you are not properly sedated, call 348 844 immediately. ***This machine has a long memory.*** There is little doubt that American fire power can win a military victory here, but to a Vietnamese peasant whose home is a lifetime of back breaking hard work, it will take more than presidential promises to convince him that we are on his side. Morley Safer, CBS News. I had bought one of these yesterday, and it doesn't fit my consumer and the

CBS News footage, Vietnam, 1965. Courtesy CBS News.

Interactive media sequence

Interactive
media sequence

THX 1138, George Lucas,
1970. Stills.

Evacuation of US embassy, Saigon, 30 April 1975.
Courtesy ABC News.

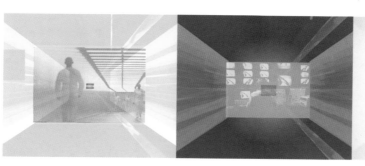

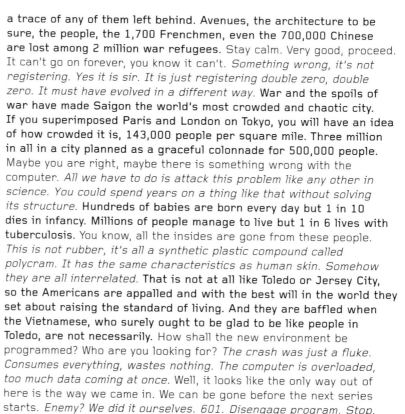

a trace of any of them left behind. Avenues, the architecture to be sure, the people, the 1,700 Frenchmen, even the 700,000 Chinese are lost among 2 million war refugees. Stay calm. Very good, proceed. It can't go on forever, you know it can't. *Something wrong, it's not registering. Yes it is sir. It is just registering double zero, double zero. It must have evolved in a different way.* War and the spoils of war have made Saigon the world's most crowded and chaotic city. If you superimposed Paris and London on Tokyo, you will have an idea of how crowded it is, 143,000 people per square mile. Three million in all in a city planned as a graceful colonnade for 500,000 people. Maybe you are right, maybe there is something wrong with the computer. *All we have to do is attack this problem like any other in science. You could spend years on a thing like that without solving its structure.* Hundreds of babies are born every day but 1 in 10 dies in infancy. Millions of people manage to live but 1 in 6 lives with tuberculosis. You know, all the insides are gone from these people. *This is not rubber, it's all a synthetic plastic compound called polycram. It has the same characteristics as human skin. Somehow they are all interrelated.* That is not at all like Toledo or Jersey City, so the Americans are appalled and with the best will in the world they set about raising the standard of living. And they are baffled when the Vietnamese, who surely ought to be glad to be like people in Toledo, are not necessarily. How shall the new environment be programmed? Who are you looking for? *The crash was just a fluke. Consumes everything, wastes nothing. The computer is overloaded, too much data coming at once.* Well, it looks like the only way out of here is the way we came in. We can be gone before the next series starts. *Enemy? We did it ourselves. 601. Disengage program. Stop.*

One and many

The subjects of Entropia – you, dear reader – are addressed in their multiplicity. That is, there are always more than one of you, especially when you are alone. The "loneliness" of its empty corridors, its furtive spaces, reverbrates with the echoes of this multiplicity. In Entropia's mirror, you come face to face with who you are not: you, alone.

The alienation of the global village, of automobility, and of airports has been tamed, emptied of its ponderous weight by the sinister, warm solicitations of belonging. Defamiliarization is familiar to the extent that it is unrecognizable. The psychosocial remains of the modern city must therefore be tracked down where they are hiding: in the living room, on the screen, in the hallway, inside, that is. And they must be remobilized, as a countermeasure to the domestication of alterity. Entropia, alienation machine, is so dedicated.

Source Material

Homeoffice

1. First City National Bank, Houston, Texas, Gordon Bunshaft of Skidmore, Owings and Merrill, 1961. Photograph © Ezra Stoller, Esto Photographics.
2. *Alphaville*, **Jean-Luc Godard, 1965.**
3. *The Trial,* Orson Welles, 1963.
4. "American Look," prod. Jam Handy Organization for General Motors Corporation (1958), courtesy Prelinger Archives, New York.
5. "Century 21 Calling," prod. Jerry Fairbanks for American Telephone & Telegraph Co. (1964), courtesy Prelinger Archives, New York.
6. "The 813 & Why", prod. Jam Handy Organization for the Xerox Corporation (1963), courtesy Prelinger Archives, New York.
7. "Frigidaire Finale," prod. Jam Handy Organization for Frigidaire, div. of General Motors Corp. (1958), courtesy Prelinger Archives, New York.
8. "Once Upon a Honeymoon," prod. Jerry Fairbanks Productions for the Bell System (1956), courtesy Prelinger Archives, New York.
9. "The Relaxed Wife," prod. On Film for J. B. Roerig and Company, division of Chas. F. Pfizer Co. (1957), courtesy Prelinger Archives, New York.
10. Printed advertisements from: *Life* (1966), *Interiors* (1961), *The Saturday Evening Post* (1963), *Look* (1953), and *Fortune* (1963).

Open House

1. Formica Corporation World's Fair House, Flushing Meadows, New York, Emil A. Schmidlin, 1964.
2. Formica Corporation, *The World's Fair House: Book of Home Styling Ideas* (Cincinnati, OH: Formica Corporation, 1964).
3. Lewin, Susan Grant, *Formica Design: From the Countertop to High Art*, (New York: Rizzoli, 1991).
4. "First Look at World's Fair Houses: A Mixture of Old and New Ideas", *House and Home*, March 1964.
5. "GH Proudly Previews a Modern Miracle: The World's Fair House", *Good Housekeeping*, Vol. 158, No. 5, May 1964, 100–113.
6. *The Graduate*, Mike Nichols, 1967.
7. *The Stepford Wives*, Bryan Forbes, 1975.
8. "A Date with Your Family", Edward C. Simmel, prod. Simmel-Meservey (1950); in Rick Prelinger, ed. *Ephemeral Films 1931–60: To New Horizons and You Can't get There from Here*, CD-Rom (New York: Voyager, 1994).

Embassy

1. United States Embassy, Saigon, Vietnam. Curtis & Davis, 1967.
2. "Ambassade des Etats-Unis a Saigon", *L'Architecture d'Aujourd'hui*, Vol. 45 No. 167, May–June 1973, 23.
3. *The Andromeda Strain, Robert Wise, 1971.*
4. *THX 1138*, George Lucas, 1970.
5. Buckley, Tom, "Foe Invades U.S. Saigon Embassy; Raiders Wiped Out After 6 Hours; Vietcong Widen Attack on Cities", *The New York Times*, 31 January, 1968.
6. Naughton, James, M. "Call For Pullout, Then a Night's Vigil at White House", *The New York Times*, 30 April 1975.
7. Arnett, Peter, "Looters Rush the Abandoned U.S. Embassy in Saigon", *The New York Times*, 1 May 1975.
8. Esper, George, "Communists Take Over Saigon; U.S. Rescue Fleet Is Picking Up Vietnamese Who Fled in Boats", *The New York Times*, 1 May 1975.
9. CBS News footage from *The War in Vietnam* (CD-Rom), prod. CBS News and *The New York Times* w/Macmillan Digital, 1995.
10. ABC News footage from *The Century of Warfare: Vietnam 1955–1989* (Videocassette), Nugus/Martin Productions, 1994.

Acknowledgements

The contribution of the following individuals to various aspects
of this work has been invaluable: Hugh Hynes, Michael Johnston,
Karen Seong, and David Winston.

Colophon

© 2001 Black Dog Publishing Limited and the authors.

Black Dog Publishing Limited PO Box 3082 London NW1 UK
T 44 (0)20 7613 1922 F 44 (0)20 7613 1944 E info@bdp.demon.co.uk

All opinions expressed in material contained within this publication
are those of the authors and not necessarily those of the publisher.

Produced by Duncan McCorquodale.
Designed by Christian Küsters.
Assisted by Owen Peyton Jones.

Printed in the European Union.

ISBN 1 901033 32 5

British Library cataloguing-in-publication data. A catalogue
record for this book is available from The British Library.

Every effort has been made to trace all copyright holders, but if any
have been inadvertently overlooked the publishers will be pleased
to make the necessary arrangements at the first opportunity.

Kadambari Baxi and Reinhold Martin are partners
in _mba_ (Martin/Baxi Architects). Kadambari Baxi is head of
the multimedia design firm imageMachine. Reinhold Martin is
an Assistant Professor of Architecture at Columbia University.

children's illustrated encyclopedia

World History

1500 - Present Day

🎵 Orpheus

First published in 2009 by Orpheus Books Ltd.,
6 Church Green, Witney, Oxfordshire OX28 4AW England
www.orpheusbooks.com

Copyright © 2009 Orpheus Books Ltd

Created and produced by Orpheus Books Ltd

Text Nicola Barber

Consultant Dr Robert Peberdy

Illustrators Simone Boni, Stephen Conlin, Giuliano
Fornari, Luigi Galante, Andrea Ricciardi di Gaudesi,
Gary Hincks, Steve Noon, Nicki Palin, Alessandro
Rabatti, Claudia Saraceni, Sergio, Thomas Trojer,
Alan Weston

ISBN 978 1 905473 50 2

A CIP record for this book is available from the British Library.

Printed and bound in Singapore

Photographs on pages 15, 19, 23, 24, 25, 26, 28, 29, 30:
The Illustrated London News Picture Library.
Photograph on page 8: © National Gallery, London

CONTENTS

RUSSIA

THE NAME RUSSIA comes from the Viking people who arrived at the town of Novgorod in the 860s. These Vikings were known as the "Varangian Rus". Some historians think that they were invited to Novgorod to sort out quarrels between the Slav peoples who lived there. Others say that the Vikings invaded. Whichever is correct, the Vikings settled in the area between Novgorod and Kiev, and it became known as the "land of the Rus".

The first ruler to bring the area under his single authority was Prince Vladimir I (ruled 980-1015). He became a Christian in 988, and made Orthodox Christianity the official religion of his new state.

Ivan the Terrible ordered the building of St. Basil's Cathedral in Moscow. Work started on it in the 1550s. It was built to celebrate Ivan's victories over the Tatars (Mongol peoples) in the southeast. St. Basil's stands inside the Kremlin *(opposite)*, a fortified citadel in the centre of Moscow.

MONGOL RULE

In 1223 Mongols attacked Russia, nearly reaching the city of Kiev. In further attacks in 1237 the Mongols sacked the city and devastated much of the land. Russia became part of the Mongol Empire, included in a region known as the "Golden Horde". The Mongols forced their subject peoples to pay heavy taxes and in 1330 they began to entrust the task of collecting these taxes to the Prince of Moscow, Ivan I. At around the same time, the leader of the Orthodox Christian Church in Russia made Moscow his main centre. Kiev declined as the power of Moscow increased.

The Mongols' control over the Golden Horde grew weaker in the 1300s. In 1380 an army led by Prince Dmitri of Moscow defeated the Mongols at Kulikovo, near the River Don. A century later (in 1480), under the rule of Ivan III, Mongol power in Russia finally came to an end. Ivan declared himself "Czar of all Russia", using the Slav version of the name of the Roman emperor, Caesar. From this time, all Russian leaders were known as czars (or tsars).

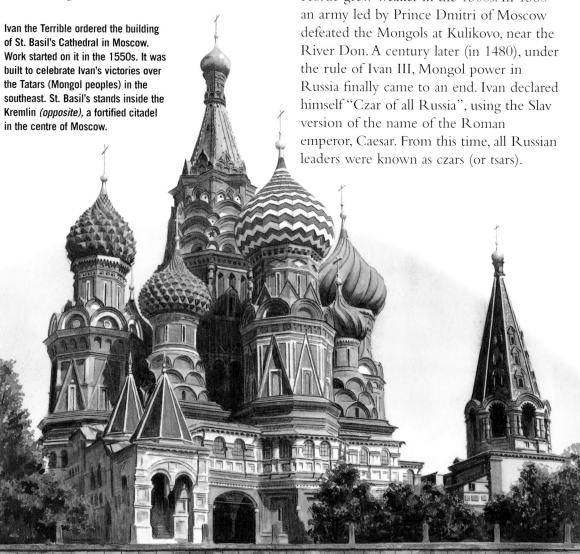

Ivan the Terrible was the grandson of Ivan III (known as "Ivan the Great"). He became renowned for his cruelty. During his reign of terror, he ordered the murder of anyone he considered a threat. He even killed his own son in a fit of rage, in 1581.

The Cossacks *(right)* were famed for their riding skills and bravery in battle. The word Cossack means "adventurer".

IVAN THE TERRIBLE

Ivan IV (ruled 1533-84) was the first Russian ruler to be crowned czar, in 1547. The power of the new czar extended across all of Russia, and his brutality was soon being felt by many of his subjects, earning him the name "Ivan the Terrible". In 1565 Ivan set up a special police force in order to break the power of the Russian nobility. Noble landowners were thrown off their estates, and many were murdered. Ivan gave these estates to his officials. Many people fled from the area around Moscow.

After the death of Ivan the Terrible, Russia entered a period known as the "Time of Troubles", when civil wars and invasions rocked the whole of Russia.

THE ROMANOVS

The Time of Troubles came to end in 1613 after the defeat of Polish invaders, and the election of Michael Romanov as the new czar. The Romanov czars were to rule Russia for the next 300 years. One of the most famous czars was Peter the Great (ruled 1682-1725). He founded the city of St. Petersburg in 1703. He also did much to reorganize the government of Russia, introducing many Western ideas.

During the rule of Catherine the Great (ruled 1762-1796) Russia's empire expanded further. But most ordinary Russians were serfs (peasants) living in terrible poverty. An uprising in the 1770s was put down by the government with great severity. Afterwards, Catherine increased control over the serfs even further.

VOYAGES OF EXPLORATION

IN 1492 Christopher Columbus (1451-1506) sailed west across the Atlantic Ocean. His aim was to find a sea route to the rich lands of the Far East—the lands of spices and silks. These lands were known to Europeans as the Indies. When Columbus set foot on one of the Caribbean islands he was convinced that he had found the Indies. He called the local people that he met "Indians". To this day, the Caribbean islands are known as the "West Indies".

HENRY THE NAVIGATOR

Prince Henry of Portugal, known as "Henry the Navigator", played a large part in directing Portuguese exploration in the 1400s. The Portuguese designed a new type of ship, called the caravel, which could withstand the ocean waves, yet was very easy to manoeuvre. Instruments such as the astrolabe also helped sailors to find their way with more accuracy.

Columbus's fleet was made up of three ships, the *Niña*, the *Pinta* and the *Santa Maria*. He made three later voyages, exploring the Caribbean coasts of Central and South America.

TRADE ROUTES

Luxury goods such as jewels, silks and spices had long been imported into Europe from the East along the Silk Road. But such overland routes had fallen under control of the Turks. In the 1400s both the Portuguese and the Spanish became interested in finding an alternative sea route to the riches of the East.

PORTUGUESE VOYAGES

Between 1424 and 1434 Prince Henry the Navigator sent many expeditions to explore the west coast of Africa. He wanted to find the source of the gold that was brought by Muslim traders north across the Sahara. In 1487 a Portuguese sailor called Bartholomeu Dias became the first European to sail around the southernmost tip of Africa, the Cape of Good Hope. He turned back soon after rounding the Cape, and arrived back in Portugal in 1488. Ten years later, Vasco da Gama went even further. He sailed around the Cape of Good Hope, up the east coast of Africa and reached India in 1498. He made a second voyage in 1502.

The Chinese explorer Zheng He made seven expeditions between 1405 and 1433. He explored as far as the east coast of Africa in a junk, a Chinese ship.

In 1519 five ships set sail from Spain. They were commanded by Ferdinand Magellan. He planned to sail down the coast of South America and round its southern-most tip. His aim was to sail west to find a route to the Spice Islands in the Far East, for the eastwards route around Africa was forbidden to Spanish ships. In fact, Magellan's fleet became the first to sail right around the world, although Magellan himself was killed in the Philippines.

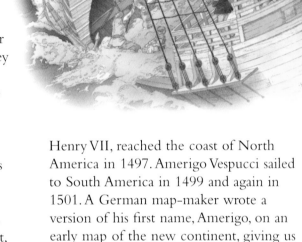

THE "NEW WORLD"

The Italian sailor Christopher Columbus tried to persuade the Portuguese to pay for a voyage across the Atlantic Ocean, but they refused. Eventually his 1492 voyage was sponsored by Queen Isabella of Spain. The Spanish were very excited by Columbus's discovery, and they paid for three more voyages under his command. However, European interest in the "New World" was to have a terrible outcome for the native peoples of the Americas *(see pages 20-21)*.

Other sailors also set out to explore this "New World". Another Italian, John Cabot, sailing in the service of the English king

Henry VII, reached the coast of North America in 1497. Amerigo Vespucci sailed to South America in 1499 and again in 1501. A German map-maker wrote a version of his first name, Amerigo, on an early map of the new continent, giving us the name "America".

Spanish invaders, known as "conquistadors" (conquerors) arrive in the Americas. Two famous conquistadors were Hernan Cortes (1485-1547) and Francisco Pizarro (1475-1541). Cortes conquered the Aztec Empire, while the Inca Empire fell to Pizarro. The Spanish claimed the "New World" for themselves and quickly established colonies there, often using brutal force. The local peoples were forced to work on their plantations. The Spanish also brought with them European diseases, such as smallpox, that were previously unknown to the local peoples. Native Americans had no immunity to these diseases, and epidemics swept through their populations, killing many thousands.

REFORMATION

ON 31st October 1517 a German monk called Martin Luther nailed a document on to the door of the Castle Church in Wittenberg. The document, known as the Ninety-five Theses, contained a series of attacks on the corruption of the Roman Catholic Church. Luther's act of protest marked the beginning of a religious movement called the Reformation.

CHURCH CORRUPTION

By the time of the Renaissance *(see pages 8-9),* the Roman Catholic Church was extremely powerful throughout Europe. Its centre was in Rome, where the pope and his court lived in lavish style. Many people thought that the Church had become corrupt, for example in its practices of offering important positions within the Church, or of selling "indulgences" (pardons

A soldier in the Thirty Years' War (1618-48), a conflict between Protestant and Catholic states in Europe.

from sins), for money. These abuses were attacked by humanist scholars such as the Dutch priest, Desiderius Erasmus. But it was Luther's protest that started the process that eventually led to a split in the Roman Catholic Church.

Although Luther had no intention of breaking with the Catholic Church when he first demanded his reforms, he was excommunicated (thrown out) of the Church by the pope in 1521. Nevertheless, he received support for his reforms from some rulers in Germany. It was during this time that the word Protestant began to be used to describe those "protesting" against the Catholic Church. The Protestant movement spread across Germany, and into Sweden and Denmark. In Switzerland it was taken up by a priest called Ulrich Zwingli who worked in Zürich.

Martin Luther posts his Ninety-five Theses on the door of the Castle Church in Wittenberg. He believed that people were saved by faith alone.

The Escorial in Spain was built by Philip II, a supporter of the Counter-Reformation.

Another reformer, called John Calvin, lived in Geneva in Switzerland. He worked to establish Protestantism in France, where his followers became known as Huguenots. Calvin's teachings were taken further afield to Scotland by John Knox.

THE ANGLICAN CHURCH

England broke with the Catholic Church for its own reasons. King Henry VIII wished to divorce his first wife, Catherine of Aragon. When the pope refused to grant the divorce, Henry broke with the Church in 1534, having already become the head of the Church in England in 1531. Later, during the reign of Edward VI, the Protestant Church in England became known as the Anglican Church.

COUNTER-REFORMATION

As Protestantism spread across Europe, the Catholic Church began to fight back with a movement known as the Counter-Reformation. There was reform within the Church, and many of the old abuses were wiped out. Catholic priests went out among the people and campaigned against Protestantism. The Catholic Church still remained very powerful, particularly in Spain and Italy. But the split between Catholics and Protestants in Europe led to persecution and conflict. In 1572 thousands of Huguenots were murdered by French Catholics in the St. Bartholomew's Day Massacre. Religious wars continued during the following centuries.

A Spanish war galleon of the 16th century. England and Spain went to war in 1588, when Spain, under Philip II, attempted to invade England. But the Spanish Armada (fleet) was wrecked by storms around Britain.

COLONIES AND COMMERCE

THE VOYAGES of exploration of the 16th century *(see pages 6-7)* opened up new possibilities to countries in Europe. Spain and Portugal began to establish colonies and trading posts in the lands discovered by their sailors. Spain took control of large areas of land in the Caribbean, as well as Central and South America. Portugal set up trading posts along the coasts of Africa and India. They were soon joined by Holland, France and Britain, who also began to lay claim to trading ports and other possessions overseas.

Black African captives were often chained together and forced to walk to the slave ports on the West African coast.

The Spanish colonists planted sugar cane plants in plantations, where they forced the local Indians to work. But so many of the local people died, from ill-treatment and from disease epidemics *(see page 7),* that there was soon a shortage of labourers. In the early 1500s the first captives were brought from Africa to the Americas to work as slaves on the plantations. The trickle soon turned to a flood, as thousands of people were transported across the Atlantic Ocean. Many died on the journey from the terrible conditions on board ship.

Founded by the Dutch, the settlement of New Amsterdam was taken over by the British in 1664 and renamed New York.

THE SLAVE TRADE

Spanish colonists in the Caribbean quickly discovered that sugar cane grew well in the hot, humid climate of the islands. Sugar was a increasingly popular in Europe, particularly as it could be used to sweeten the new drinks that were also arriving from overseas colonies—coffee, tea and cocoa.

WEALTH AND PROFIT

Overseas colonies brought huge wealth to countries in Europe. Spain plundered its colonies on the American mainland, importing vast amounts of gold and silver. Portugal, too, had rich sources of gold in its colony in Brazil. Goods such as sugar (from the Caribbean), tea (from China), coffee and chocolate (from South America) also became increasingly popular across Europe.

The slave trade was another source of vast wealth. The slave trade between Africa and America is known as the "triangular trade" because it was made up of three stages. Ships sailed to Africa from Europe loaded with goods to exchange for slaves—guns and alcohol, for example. Captives were then transported across the Atlantic. In the Caribbean, the captives were sold and the money used to buy sugar, rum and tobacco which was then taken back to Europe. Britain became one of the leaders of the slave trade, but other European countries such as France, Holland and Portugal also took part in this terrible trade. In Britain, the ports of London, Liverpool and Bristol flourished as the profits poured in.

Pirates attack a treasure-carrying Spanish galleon in the Caribbean Sea in the 1600s.

TRADE WITH CHINA

Although the Chinese were happy to export goods such as silks and spices to the West, they rigorously controlled imports into their country. Foreigners were allowed to trade through one port only, Guangzhou.

World trade received a boost with the opening of the Suez Canal in 1869. The canal created a shortcut between the Mediterranean Sea and Red Sea.

In the 19th century British merchants in China tried to get round these restrictions by illegally importing the drug, opium. They were backed by the British government, resulting in the Opium Wars between Britain and China (1839-42, 1856-60). China was forced to back down and accept European trade in its territories.

The British steamship *Nemesis* attacks Chinese junks (ships) during the Opium Wars. Opium is a drug that is made from the juice of the opium poppy. It is dangerous because it is addictive. Opium addiction was a serious problem in China in the 18th and 19th centuries.

THE AGE OF REVOLUTION

IN THE second half of the 18th century two major revolutions took place. The first was in North America (1775-83), and it led to the birth of the United States of America. The second happened in France, starting with the storming of the Bastille Prison in Paris in 1789.

REVOLUTION IN AMERICA

From the early 16th century onwards, North America had been settled by groups of colonists from various European countries. During the Seven Years' War (1756-63), British and French colonists fought over territory in North America.

The guillotine was the main method of execution during the French Revolution. Thousands of people suspected of being hostile to the government were beheaded during the "Reign of Terror" 1793-94.

Britain emerged victorious, with control of a vast area of land. By this time there were 13 British colonies in North America (apart from Canada). The colonists were under British rule, but had no say in how they were governed. During the years after the war, the British government imposed many different taxes on the colonists. These taxes provoked protests against what the colonists called "taxation without representation". The first shots between British troops and American colonists were fired in Lexington, Massachusetts on 19th April 1775, marking the opening of the war. In July 1776 the colonists issued the Declaration of Independence and the United States of America was born. The end of the war came in 1783, when British troops surrendered at Yorktown, Virginia.

On 14th July 1789 a Parisian mob stormed the royal prison in the capital, the Bastille. Although there were few prisoners in the prison, the storming of the prison seriously weakened the authority and power of the French king, Louis XIV. At the same time, riots broke out across the country. The French Revolution had begun. The king, Louis XIV and his wife, Marie-Antoinette, tried to escape, but they were arrested. The National Assembly abolished the monarchy in 1792. The king was tried and executed on the guillotine in January 1793. Marie-Antoinette followed him to the guillotine in October of the same year.

A meeting of leaders of the American colonists in the Second Continental Congress in July 1775. The Congress issued the Declaration of Independence, drawn up by Thomas Jefferson, which asserted the independence of the American colonies from Britain. The Declaration was not recognized by Britain until the signing of the Treaty of Paris in 1783 after the end of the war in which British forces were defeated by American troops commanded by George Washington.

THE FRENCH REVOLUTION

In France, discontent about taxation was also growing amongst the ordinary people in the late 18th century. At that time, neither clergy nor noble families in France paid any taxes. The burden of taxation fell on working people and peasants. In 1788 a bad harvest meant that many people were close to starvation. The country was almost bankrupt as a result of costly wars and the extravagant lifestyle of the monarchy. When the king refused to listen to the demands of the people, they formed the National Assembly. At the same time, unrest was growing in the streets and on 14th July 1789 a mob attacked the royal prison in Paris, the Bastille. This event marked the beginning of the French Revolution.

On 26th August the National Assembly made a Declaration of the Rights of Man, giving the same basic rights to all citizens, including liberty and equality. Soon, France was also at war with many other European nations. A general called Napoleon Bonaparte had risen quickly through the ranks of the French army. In 1799 he seized power in France and began his campaign to conquer the rest of Europe.

One of the many battles of the Napoleonic Wars (1799-1815). Napoleon built an empire which covered much of Europe by 1812. He was finally defeated at the Battle of Waterloo in June 1815.

NATIVE AMERICANS

WHEN the first Europeans arrived in North America in the 16th century, they found the land occupied by tribes of Native Americans. These local people had lived there for generations, developing their own cultures and ways of life. The arrival of Europeans changed the Native Americans' lives for ever. Imported diseases *(see page 7)* spread like wildfire through the local peoples, killing millions. Many more were killed in land disputes with the European colonists.

During the 19th century European settlers poured into the United States of America and the country expanded westwards *(see pages 22-23)*. At first, the American government set aside some areas of land for the Native Americans, known as "reservations". Then, in 1830, the government passed the Indian Removal Act which gave it the right to force Native Americans to move from their homelands on to land in the West that the European settlers did not want.

Warriors of the Sioux tribe prepared for battle by dancing together to draw on the power of the "Great Spirit" *(below)*. Many warriors painted an image of a powerful beast on to their shields, to strengthen themselves for battle.

Sioux chiefs *(above),* such as Sitting Bull, wore impressive eagle-feather headdresses as a sign of their great bravery. Sitting Bull was the leader of the Sioux at the time of their victory at the Battle of Little Bighorn. He was killed by American troops in 1890.

The people of the Great Plains lived in tipis, tents made from buffalo hides stretched over wooden poles. After Europeans introduced the horse into North America in the 16th century, the Native Americans of the Plains became skilful riders, using horses to help them hunt the herds of buffalo that lived on the Plains. Buffalo provided the Plains peoples with meat for food, as well as hides for clothing and shelter. When the herds of buffalo were destroyed in the 19th century, the Native Americans' way of life was destroyed, too.

Abraham Lincoln v
from 1861-5, duri
War. He helped to

THE GOLD F

In January 1848 a r
Marshall was inspec
sawmill when he n
glittering in the wa
picked it up. It was
discovery of gold in
out. People came fi
and many parts of
fortunes in the gol
travelled overland a
others came by sea
few made any mor

FIGHTING FOR THE LAND

Most Native Americans did not want to move from their traditional homelands, and fought bitterly against the American government. In the southeast, for example, the Cherokee were forced off their lands by government troops and forced to walk thousands of kilometres to reservations in the West. Thousands died, and this journey became known as "The Trail of Tears". The Native Americans of the Plains also fought the settlers who moved into their territories. But their old ways of life were destroyed when hunters almost completely wiped out the herds of buffalo that lived on the Great Plains. Sometimes, however, there were Native American victories over the army: for example, at the Battle of Little Bighorn (1876), when Sioux warriors defeated General Custer's troops.

THE G

AMERI

WHEN
North

they founded
coast. But afte
War (see page
west of the A
early pioneer
farmers looki

The move
the followin
President Jef
of Louisiana
Louisiana st
River to the
sent out an
Lewis and V
about his pu
reached the

AFTER THE WAR

WORLD WAR II came to an end in 1945 *(see page 29)*. Millions had died and cities around the world were left in ruins. In particular, Hitler had been determined to wipe out Jewish communities in the territories he controlled, and millions had died in slave camps and concentration camps. The terrible death and destruction inspired people to ensure that such a war could never happen again. In 1945 50 nations signed the charter of the United Nations, promising to promote world peace.

The Soviet leader, Joseph Stalin *(right)*, US President Roosevelt *(centre)* and the British leader, Winston Churchill *(left)*, meet at the Yalta Conference in 1945 to discuss plans for after the end of war.

THE COLD WAR

At the end of the war, it was clear that two countries—the United States of America and the Soviet Union—had become the world's leading powers, the "superpowers". (The Soviet Union was formed in 1922 when Russia joined with other territories under Communist rule.) After the war, Soviet leaders tried to extend Communist rule in Europe and Asia. The struggle between the Communists and the Americans was known as the "Cold War".

Mohandas Karamchand Gandhi (1869-1948) led the Indian campaign for independence. He became known as Mahatma, meaning "Great Soul". He was a peace-loving man who led a campaign of non-co-operation against the British, but refused to use violence. One of his most famous protests was the Salt March of 1930, when he led hundreds of people to the sea to make salt from seawater. This was in protest at the Salt Acts imposed by the British, which forced people to buy heavily taxed salt direct from the government.

INDEPENDENCE

India had been a British territory since 1858. Despite Indian demands for reform and, after 1917, for independence, Britain was very reluctant to let India go. After the 1920s the campaign for independence was led by Mahatma Gandhi.

It was not until after World War II that the British government finally agreed to Indian independence. However, religious matters led to terrible bloodshed. Although the majority of people in India were Hindus, there were also many Muslims who did not want to live under Hindu rule. The Muslim leader Mohammed Ali Jinnah campaigned for a separate state for Muslims,

`The Communists came to power in China in 1949, under the leadership of Mao Zedong *(right)*. Mao oversaw dramatic reforms in China designed to improve the economy and increase food production. Industries were brought under government control and land was taken over by co-operatives. However, many people were killed or sent into exile for criticizing Mao.

After the war, Germany was divided up between the USA, Britain, France and the Soviet Union. The capital, Berlin, lay in the Soviet zone, but was also divided between the four powers. In 1949 three zones were joined together to form West Germany, while the Soviet zone became East Germany with a Communist government. Berlin remained divided and, in 1961, the Communists built a wall across the city to prevent people moving from East to West. The hated wall came down in 1989 *(right),* when Communism in eastern Europe collapsed.

and the British were eventually forced to agree. In 1947 two areas in northwest and northeast India became the Muslim state of Pakistan (the northeast part is present-day Bangladesh). As people moved from one state to the other, violence broke out between the two sides: thousands died. India became independent on 15th August 1947.

Many other former colonies also gained their independence after World War II. Many African colonies became independent peacefully—others were forced to fight for it. In South Africa, the white minority used a policy called "apartheid" to keep the black majority out of power. The struggle to end apartheid finally succeeded in 1994, when free elections were held and Nelson Mandela became president.

THE MODERN WORLD

The Cold War finally came to an end in the early 1990s as Communism collapsed. Today, many countries are fighting a "war on terror" after the events of 11th September 2001. US-led wars in Iraq and Afghanistan have begun since then.

There also continues to be a huge gap between rich and poor countries. Making sure everyone has food, health care and education is a major challenge for the future.

This is the same view of New York as on page 27, about 100 years later. The car has transformed life for people in the 20th century, giving them more freedom than ever before, but it has also introduced new problems. Pollution from exhaust fumes is a major problem in most cities. Air pollution is also a cause of global warming, which could affect the climate patterns of the Earth.

INDEX

Page numbers in **bold** refer to main entries.